This SUPER AWESOME Bool

Winner of the Art Competition

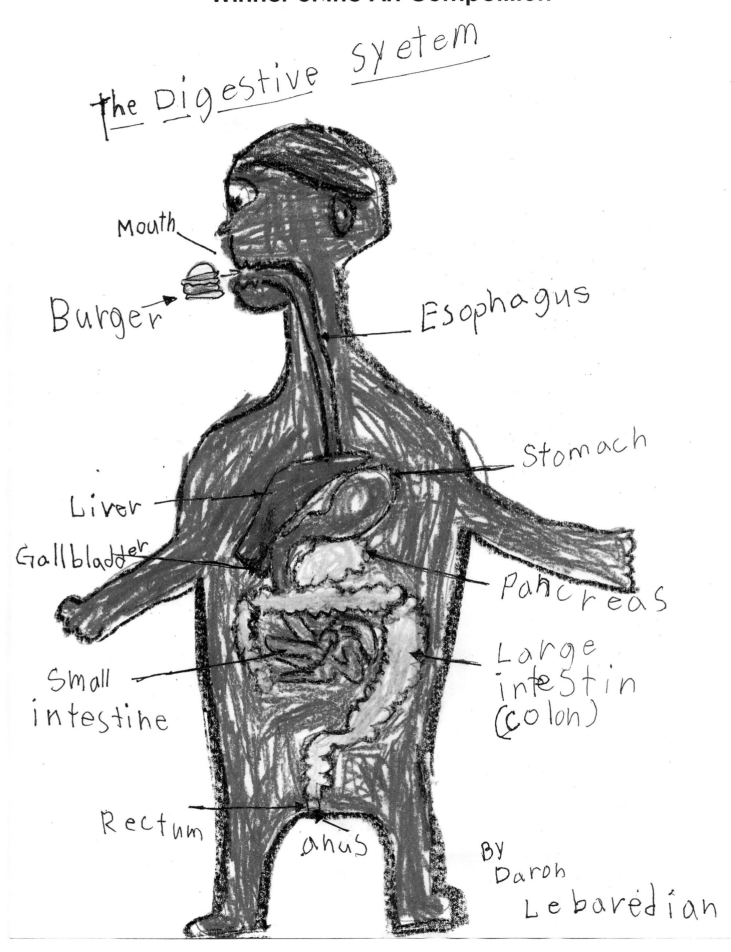

The Digestive Syetem

Mouth

Burger

Esophagus

Stomach

Liver

Gallbladder

Pancreas

Small intestine

Large intestin (colon)

Rectum

anus

BY Daron Lebaredian

ANATOMY and Physiology PART 2:
Body Systems

By:
April Chloe Terrazas

This book is dedicated to:

Elias & Diana Urbina, whose love and support I will cherish forever.

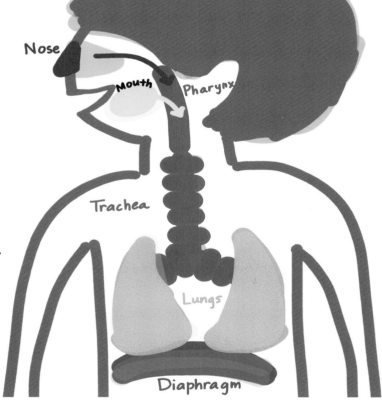

Nose

Mouth

Pharynx

Trachea

Lungs

Diaphragm

Anatomy & Physiology PART 2: Body Systems
April Chloe Terrazas, BS University of Texas at Austin.
Copyright © 2014 Crazy Brainz, LLC

Visit us on the web! www.Crazy-Brainz.com
Cover design, illustrations and text by: April Chloe Terrazas

Body systems are groups of organs that work together for your body to function properly. Right now, you are using all of your body systems!

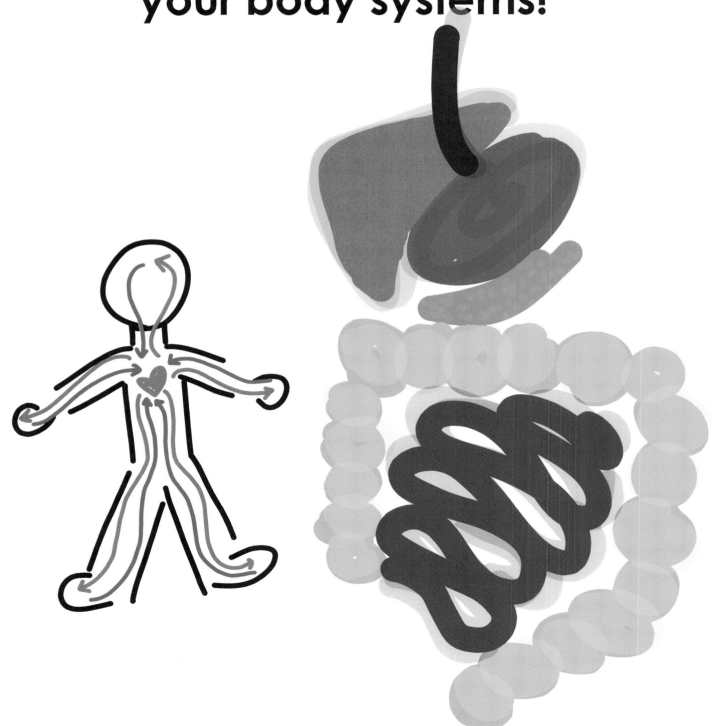

Are you ready to learn about body systems?

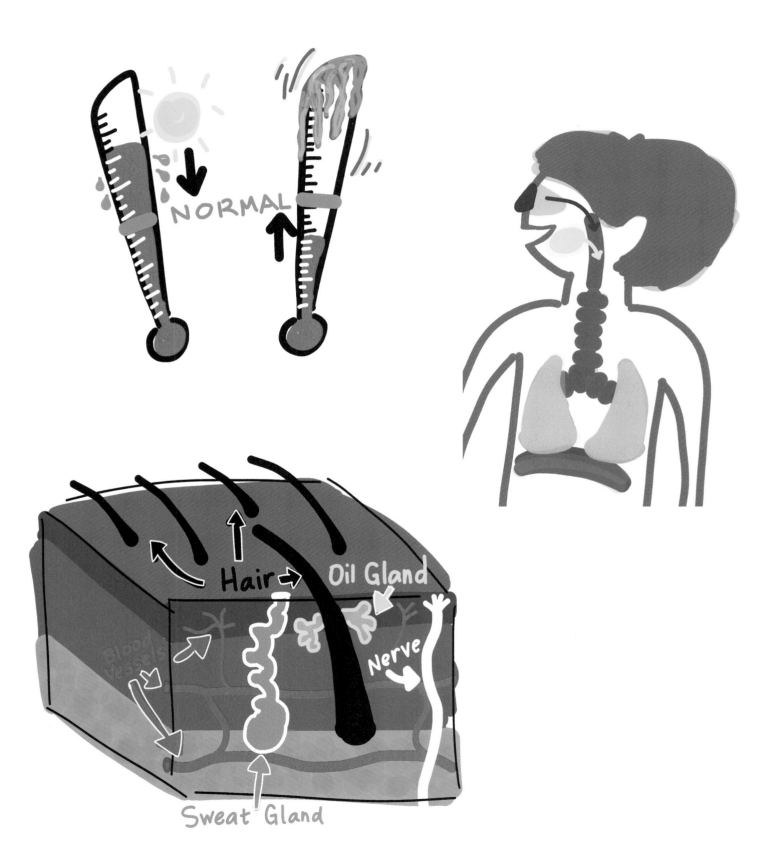

Circulatory System

Sound it Out
1. SER
2. Q
3. LUH
4. TOR
5. EE

The circulatory system is a network of vessels throughout your body. They are everywhere!

The circulatory system is like a railroad. It moves blood and chemicals all over the body.

The main station on the circulatory system railroad is the heart!

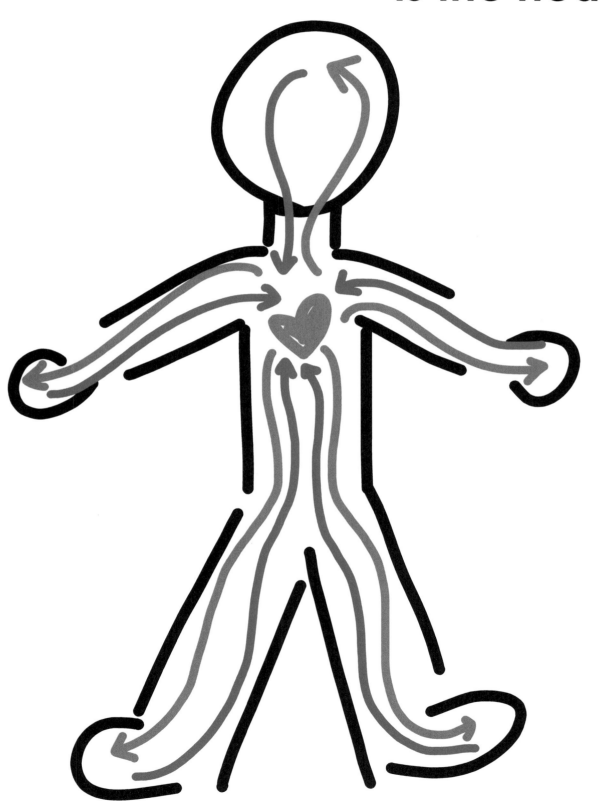

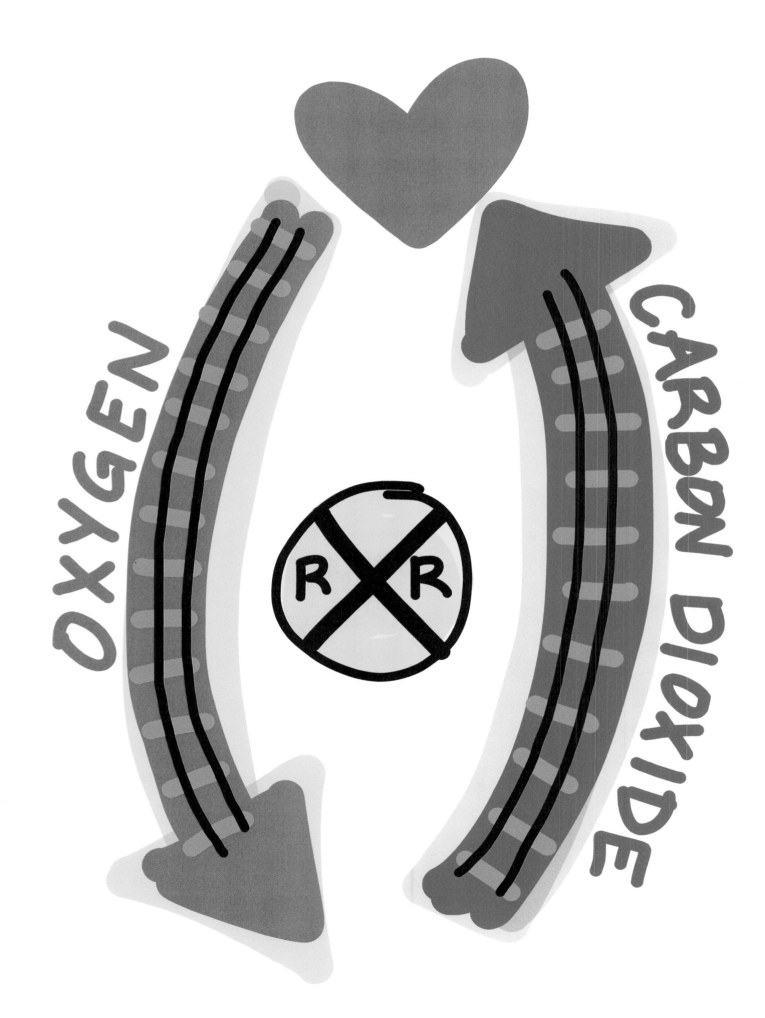

The circulatory system railroad goes to every organ in the body.

All of the cells in our body need oxygen to survive.

The circulatory system is connected with all of our cells and delivers oxygen.

Take a deep breath...
...and let it out.

Your circulatory system took oxygen from the lungs and gave back CO_2 to be exhaled.

Respiratory System

Sound it Out
1. RES
2. PI
3. RUH
4. TOR
5. EE

The respiratory system works with the circulatory system.

Oxygen is breathed in through the respiratory system and from there is transferred to the blood in the circulatory system.

Then the circulatory system delivers oxygen to all of your cells and comes back to the lungs to transfer CO_2 out of the body.

Take a deep breath...

...let it out.

Oxygen was transferred into the blood stream (circulatory system) and carbon dioxide was transferred out of the blood stream and breathed out through the respiratory system.

The respiratory system is made of the following parts:

Nose: NOZ

Mouth: MOWTH

Pharynx: FAR-INX

Trachea: TRA-KEE-UH

Lungs: LUNGZ

Diaphragm: DI-UH-FRAM

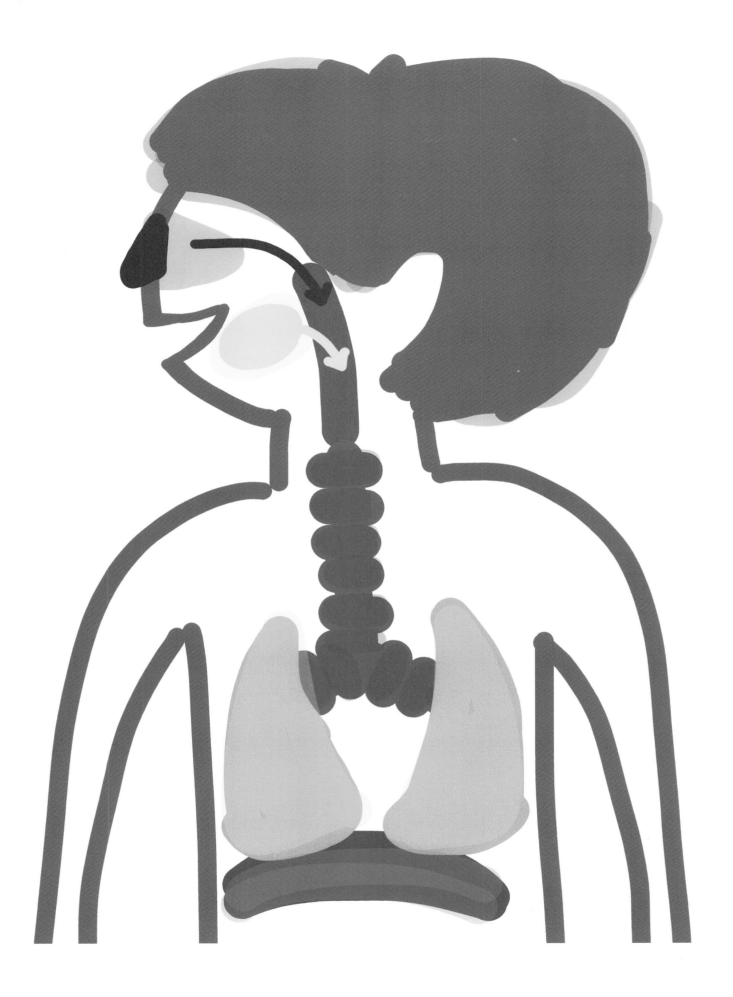

We need oxygen to survive. We especially need it to be active and play!

When you run very fast, what happens to your breathing?

Oxygen is coming in faster and CO_2 is going out faster.

Oxygen goes in the nose or mouth, through the pharynx, down the trachea, and into the lungs. Air is pushed in and out of the lungs by the diaphragm.

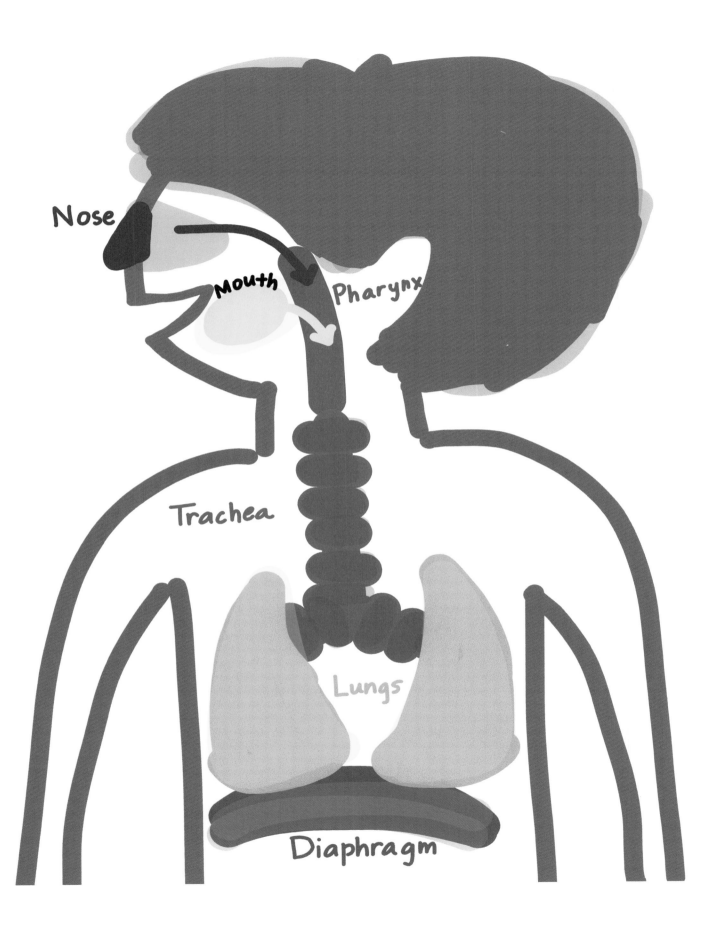

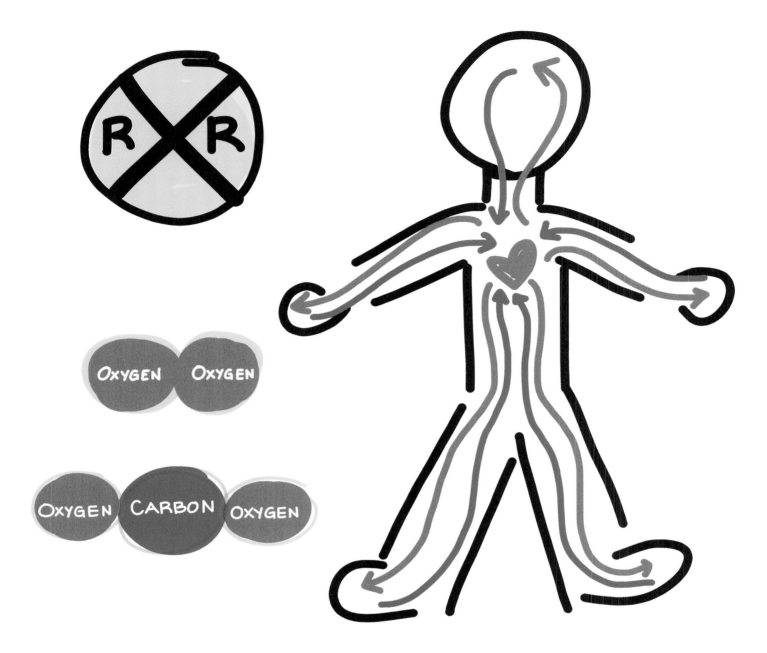

The **circulatory system** is like a railroad, delivering oxygen and chemicals to all cells in the body and taking carbon dioxide out of the body.
The main station is the heart.

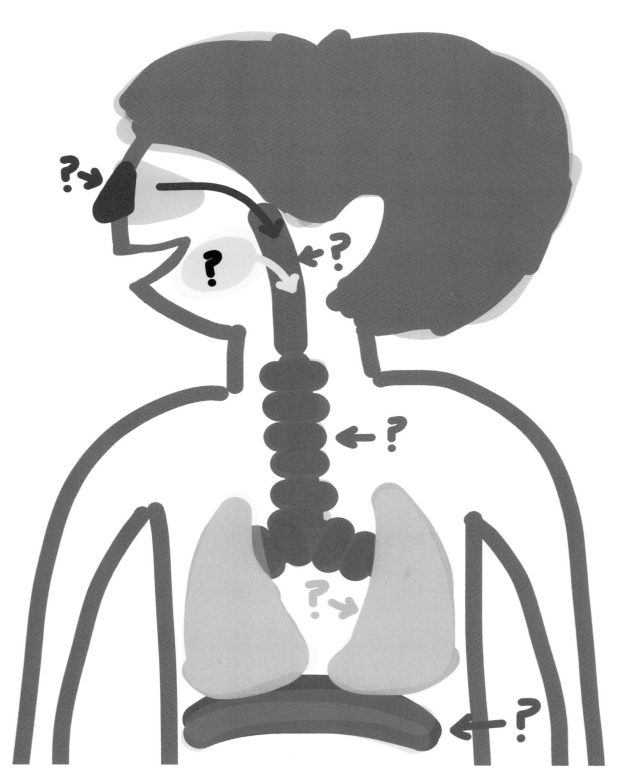

The respiratory system works with the circulatory system. The respiratory system takes in oxygen and releases CO_2.

Digestive System

Sound it Out
1. DI
2. JES
3. TIV

DO YOU LIKE TO EAT?

The digestive system takes in food, digests (or breaks down) the food, absorbs the nutrients we need to be healthy and eliminates the stuff we do not need.

Digestion begins when you chew your food.

This is called **mechanical** digestion.

Mechanical

Sound it Out

1. MEH
2. KAN
3. EH
4. KUL

You are using something, (your teeth), to physically break down the food.

Your mouth releases enzymes to help break down food while you are chewing. This enzyme in the mouth is called amylase.

This is called chemical digestion.

Chemical digestion continues in the stomach.

Enzymes

Sound it Out

1. IN
2. ZIMZ

Chemical digestion uses chemicals (enzymes) to break down food in the mouth and in the stomach.

Chemical

Sound it Out

1. KIM
2. EH
3. KUL

Esophagus: E - SOF - UH - GUS

Stomach: STUH - MUK

Small Intestine: SMALL IN - TES - TIN

Large Intestine: LARGE IN - TES - TIN

Liver: LIV - R

Pancreas: PAN - KREE - US

Abdomen: AB - DO - MIN

- -

Food enters the mouth, goes down the esophagus to the stomach. Then it goes to the small intestine and finally to the large intestine, then exits the body. Other organs in your abdomen (or stomach area) are the liver and the pancreas.

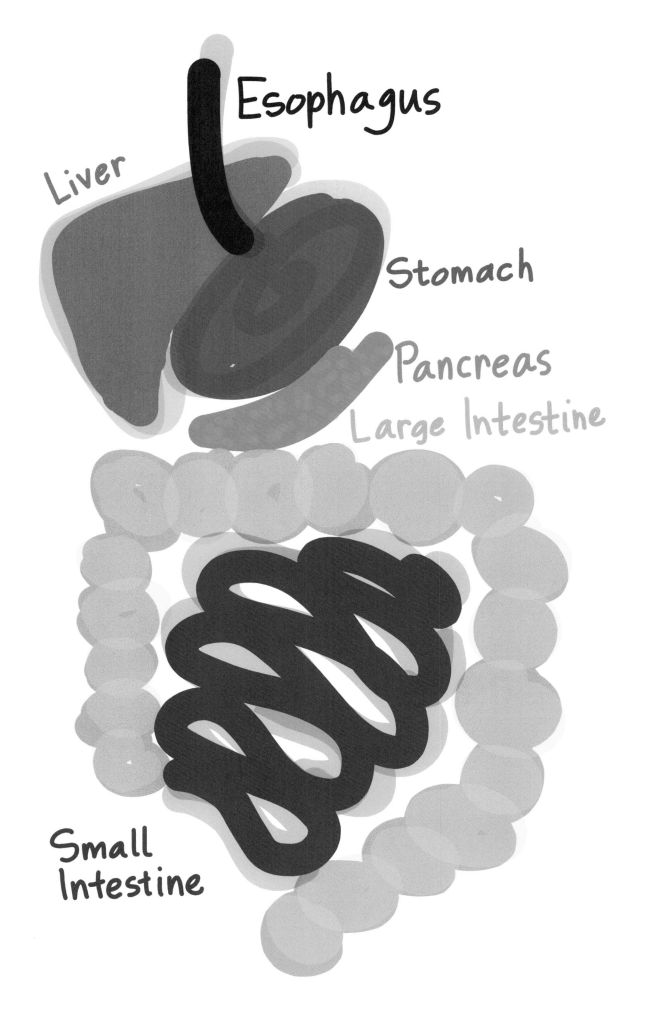

The digestive system starts in the mouth with chewing (mechanical digestion).

Chemical digestion occurs when enzymes break down food. This happens in the mouth with amylase and also in the stomach with other enzymes.

Digesting food follows this path: mouth, esophagus, stomach, small intestine, large intestine, and then out of the body.

Integumentary System

The integumentary system is your skin, hair and nails. It protects your organs from damage and disease. It also helps regulate (or keep normal) your body temperature.

The integumentary system regulates body temperature by sweating to cool your body and shivering to warm your body.

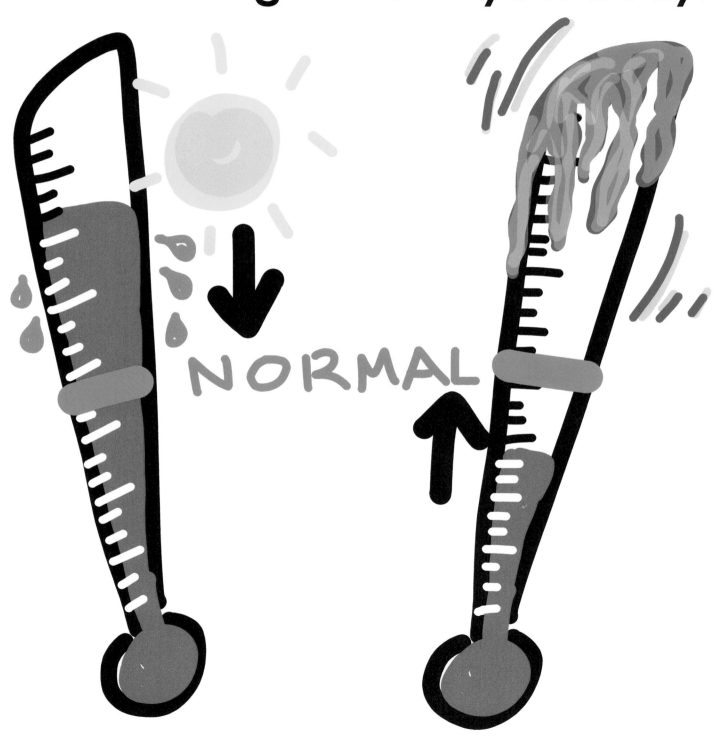

NORMAL

The integumentary system is made of your skin, nails and hair.

Skin is a type of epithelial.

Epithelial

Sound it Out

1. EP
2. EH
3. THEE
4. LEE
5. UL

Epithelials cover your outer body surfaces and also line internal organs, protecting them from harm.

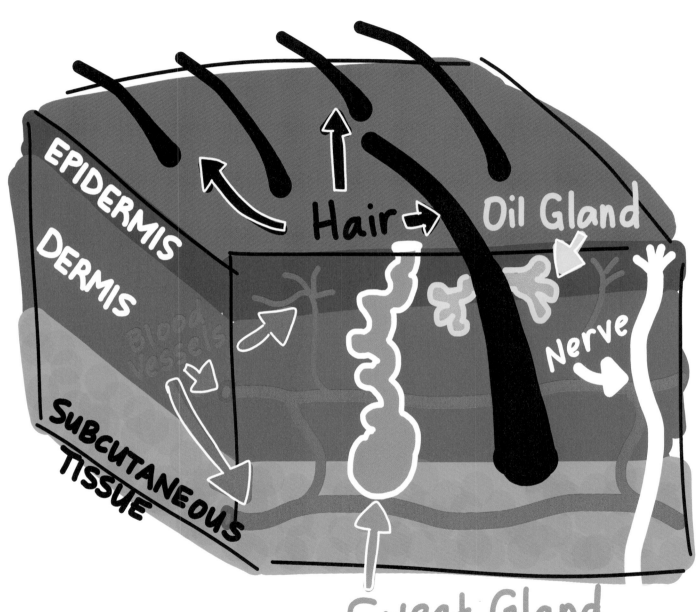

Immune System

Your immune system **protects your body from invaders!**

*Have you ever had a cough or a runny nose***?**

That is your immune system **working to fight off invaders.**

The immune system works with the integumentary and circulatory systems.

The skin (integumentary system) is like a shield and the circulatory system is like a sword.

The immune system releases fighters into your blood stream (circulatory system) to attack invaders that get past the shield.

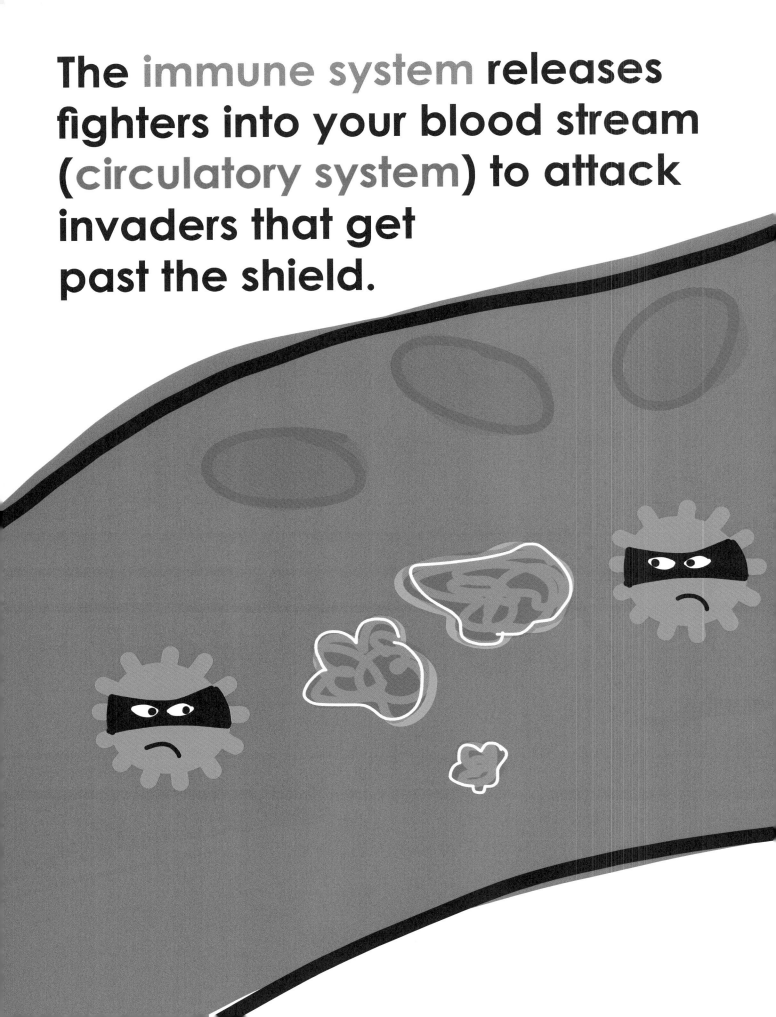

Circulatory System

Blood cells

The **immune system** works together with the integumentary system and **circulatory system** to protect your body from invaders.

Skin, hair and nails are all part of the integumentary system.

Skin is a type of epithelial.

The integumentary system **regulates body temperature.**

The **immune system** keeps you healthy by fighting off invaders.

If a foreign object gets past the skin or into the blood stream (circulatory system), the immune system sends out fighters to destroy the foreign invaders!

QUESTIONS:

What is the circulatory system?

What is the main station of the circulatory system?

The circulatory system brings _____ to all cells in the body and takes _____ out of the body.

What is the respiratory system?

What are the six parts of the respiratory system?

What is the digestive system?

What is the difference between mechanical and chemical digestion?

What is amylase?

Name the parts of the digestive system.

What is the integumentary system?

What is the immune system?

What happens when invaders get into the circulatory system?

VERY GOOD!!!

Circulatory system

Respiratory system

Digestive system

Mechanical **digestion**

Chemical **digestion**

Integumentary system

Immune system

Nose

Mouth

Pharynx

Trachea

Lungs

Diaphragm

Enzymes

Esophagus

Stomach

Small Intestine

Large Intestine

Liver

Pancreas

Abdomen

Epithelial

Draw YOUR body systems!

CPSIA information can be obtained
at www.ICGtesting.com
Printed in the USA
LVIC06n1156151214
418898LV00006B/8